# WINNING
*is*
# PLANNED

## HOW TO COUNT THE WINS AND KEEP WINNING

*For Young Ladies and Women Who Plan Their Success*

## Dr. Jessica K. Ellis & Dr. Stanley K. Ellis

SILLE
EDUCATIONAL FOUNDATION

First Printing, 2021
ISBN 979-8-9851737-0-3
P.O. Box 165032
Little Rock, AR 72116
www.mie4success.org

*When we are raised to be our true authentic selves, we are given permission to live our best lives.*

-JESSICA K. ELLIS,
*Businesswoman & Investor*

*This journal is dedicated to my father, the best girl dad, who encouraged me to be myself and to march to the beat of my own drum.*

MR. CHESTER DENE SMITH
January 30, 1950—March 9, 2021

*For the Spirit God gave us does not make us timid, but gives us power, love and self-discipline.*

**2 Timothy 1:7**

# GOOD DAY LADIES!

I am thrilled you have made a conscious decision to open this journal. I applaud you for your courage to engage with such a book and I encourage you to be diligent, steadfast, and true to the work that you do inside these pages...and *inside your mind, body and spirit*. The pressures and demands placed on young ladies and women by society, social media, our parents, our spouses and our employers are plentiful. These pressures and demands often lead to self-care and dream achievement being placed at the bottom of our priority list. To realize our Success in life, it is imperative that we commit to making ourselves priority #1. With that said, I want you to go to the nearest mirror and say the following statement aloud five times with the utmost confidence: **"Today I make a commitment to myself to make ME priority #1"**. Welcome back from the mirror. Now, write this statement on a sticky note and place it on the mirror you use to get ready each morning. Every morning, for 66 days, I challenge and encourage you to read your commitment message aloud as you look into your own eyes.

In this journal, you will have the opportunity to re-prioritize your daily routines to ensure you not only have time to plan your wins but also exercise self-care. (*Secret:* Practicing self-care is a WIN.) Each day you will have the opportunity to make yourself priority #1.

This journal has been developed specifically with you in mind to help you define your Success while also Motivating, Inspiring, and Empowering you to achieve whatever goals you set for yourself. Just like most things in life that are worth attaining, Success is a process. To enjoy your Success, you have to enjoy the process. I like to call this the M.I.E. process. To help you understand what you should be doing in this journal and why you should be doing it, let us begin by defining Success and the process of **M**otivation, **I**nspiration, and **E**mpowerment that will get you there.

## Success in 66:

We all have habits. Some of them are good and some are not so good. Some of our habits we are very proud of and others, well…not so much. What I would like for you to realize at this point in your journal is that none of your not-so-good habits will help you achieve the Success you want and deserve. **Brace yourself!** Some of your good habits will not help you achieve your Success either. Shocked? I was as well. Just because the habit is "good" does not mean that it will help you achieve your goals. To achieve your goals, the habits you build **MUST** be focused on and lead to the Success you desire. For example, you have a habit of waking at 5:00 a.m. each weekday to meditate before your family wakes. However, your goal is to increase your workouts over time from 30 minutes at least three times a week to an hour at least four days per week. Your good habit of waking at 5:00 a.m. to meditate before your family wakes WILL NOT lead to you increasing your workouts over time from 30 minutes at least three times a week to an hour at least four days per week. Your habits have to be focused towards your goals for you to achieve them.

Some experts say that it takes 66 days to develop a habit. Other experts tell us that to become Successful, we have to develop good habits and get rid of bad habits (or learn to manage them better). In essence, you are here to develop good behaviors that will become natural to you. You will begin to do these things with the regularity and consistency that you exhibit with simple things like brushing your teeth, tying your shoes or combing your hair. Okay, maybe combing your hair takes a little more thought, but you get the picture. I have developed this journal you currently hold in your hand to help you start your journey to Success. This journal will help you build good habits… **in 66 days**…that focus directly on you achieving your goals.

## The Look of Success:

Everyone defines Success differently and that is to be expected. Some see Success as having a husband with two and a half children while others see it as having a big house or their dream career. Many think they will have achieved "Success" when they accomplish or achieve the goal that they have set for themselves. In actuality, none of these things define what Success really is. Most people see Success as a destination. A place you get to and stop. In all actuality, Success is *the pursuit of a worthy goal or goals.* Success comes from going after what it is you want. Success is the process. To be truly Successful, you must learn to enjoy the process, the pursuit of your goals. If you cannot learn to be happy while you are on the journey towards your goal, you will not be happy when you reach it. Let us be clear, if you have a worthy goal and you are going after it, you are already Successful. If you learn to enjoy the pursuit of your goal, your happiness will last much longer than when you reach it. The first step is to identify your Motivation.

## The Truth About Motivation:

Most people think motivation is the excitement you get or feel about your goal. People often confuse motivation with feeling good or being excited about something. Feeling good and being excited is something else altogether. I will explain what I mean in the next paragraph. For now, let us focus on Motivation. Motivation is your reason for having your goal in the first place. Your goal may be to have a really big house one day. Your reason could be you want to give your mother the home she never had, or perhaps you want to take care of all your sisters and brothers, or maybe a big house says to you that you have "made it". Your motivation is *your reason*, *your why*. Identifying "why" you want to achieve this goal is your motivation. This is your anchor. When times get hard (**and they will**) on your journey to achieving your goal, your Motivation, your why will be what keeps you going. Your why is what makes the goal worth achieving in the first place. Step 2 is to keep yourself Inspired.

## Keeping Yourself Going:

You should certainly *have a goal that you are excited about, have enthusiasm for achieving the goal and feel good when you are working towards it.* This is what Inspiration is. The truth of the matter is that your Inspiration will come and go, but your Motivation, your "why", is the anchor that keeps you going even when you do not feel like it. People think when you are excited and fired up about your goal, you are Motivated. That is not true. Those feelings are your

Inspiration. They are as necessary as your Motivation. Both your Motivation and your Inspiration are part of a formula that will help you on your journey *of* Success. You should always try to stay inspired about your goal. Feeling good about it makes the journey that much more enjoyable but Inspiration is NOT a constant. It is not always there. Stay Inspired as much as you can. You must Inspire and re-Inspire yourself each day. The third step is to Empower yourself.

## Authorizing Your Own Success:

Empowerment is utilizing the resources at your disposal, the tools you have acquired as well as the knowledge and experiences you have gained to help you achieve your goals. Empowerment is also, *you authorizing yourself to achieve your goals*. Empowerment is you telling yourself that you have the right to the Success that you desire. This is probably the most important part of Empowerment. You have to give yourself the authority to be Successful. Only you can authorize your Success and only you can take that authorization away. You are in control. You will either Empower yourself or you will dis-Empower yourself. The first one will ensure your Success. The second will ensure your non-Success. The final step in the Success process is to **REPEAT** steps one, two and three.

# PLANNING TO WIN

S teven Covey, author of *The 7 Habits of Highly Effective People*, stated that you should begin with the end in mind. You need to know where you are going before you can plan your journey, otherwise you end up traveling without an actual destination. If you do this, you are wasting your time and could end up anywhere. **This is not the route you will want to take.** To be effective in planning to achieve your goal and Successful in reaching your destination, you will have to identify the steps between where you are right now in your life and where you want to be. There will be a lot of mini-goals or steps you will have to make before you achieve the Success goal you have identified for yourself. No woman, no team, no one wins without a plan. How well you plan will determine how fast and how much Success you enjoy. The main thing to remember is this, to achieve your Success you will have to become the person who would deserve that Success. You will have to change to become the person you are meant to be. You will have to change how you think, how you act, how you talk and perhaps how you look so that who you are lines up with who you are meant to be.

No Success will ever come to you without change on your part in some area or multiple areas of your life. The change will not always feel good but it will be necessary to achieve your goals. One of these changes may require you to seek out new friends and probably leave some of your older ones behind. It may require you to wake at 4:30 a.m. instead of your usual 6:45 a.m. You will need to seek out new information from new people. This will be scary but you will need to overcome your fear to achieve your goal. Not all of the people around you will understand why you are changing or why you even want Success. This will be a major source of discomfort for you, but once again, it will be necessary for you to become who you are meant to be and achieve the Success you deserve. You will need to make your change part of your plan to win. For 21st century young ladies and women, this means being intentional about your entire day and the activities that occur throughout your day. Sound like a lot? It is. Will it be easy? It won't. Will you do it? AbsoFREAKINlutely!

If you do not plan to win, you are planning to fail. To achieve any great Success in life you must begin with your goal in mind and lay out your plan to achieve that goal. You can look at it this way, if you were going on a trip to a different state you would plan your route to get there. Part of your plan would include buying snacks, filling your car with gas, identifying places you may stop for food along the way and places you may stop to sleep. All of this is done before you leave your home. It is all planned as part of your journey to get to your destination. This is no different from planning to achieve your Success in life. You MUST layout your plan or shall I say, write your plan out. A plan that is not written down is simply a thought. Thoughts are often fleeting and forgotten and so are the plans that are contained in those thoughts. Writing your plans down on paper helps you keep them in your mind and gives you something to refer back to if you cannot remember exactly what you said you were going to do. Written plans can also keep you Inspired as you work on achieving your goal. Just seeing your goals and plans written down on paper can give you something you can get excited about and fuel you to push forward, especially when you do not feel like it. Just like any other journey, when things happen and you have to get off the road to fix a flat tire or get more fuel, your plan is there to tell you which direction to go when you get back on the road. Things will happen in your life that will take you off the road to your goals for a moment but your plan is there to help you get back on the path to complete your journey and achieve YOUR SUCCESS.

*Write the vision and make it plain on tablets.*

HABAKKUK 2:2

# INVESTMENT VS. SACRIFICE

**M**any people talk about the sacrifices they make as if they should be praised for them. Parents are in this group. Sometimes parents like to talk about the number of sacrifices they have made for their children. Nine times out of 10 they are telling this to their children and they want praise for what they have sacrificed. Sometimes parents do not see what they have sacrificed as positive investments into their children's lives, futures and ultimately their Success. In addition, society seems to equate WOMAN (WOMEN) with sacrifice and we as women often times adopt the "sacrifice" badge as something to be honored. This is probably where the cycle of seeing the things you do in your life to succeed as sacrifices (negative) and not investments (positive).

Most people see what they do to become Successful as sacrifice. If they save their money to buy real estate, purchase stock in the stock market, or start a business, you will hear them say, "I sacrificed to do this". Really what they are considering a sacrifice should be viewed as an INVESTMENT towards achieving the Success they want. Today, as you read this book and begin your work on you and your goals, I encourage you to see everything you do to achieve your goals as an

INVESTMENT that is getting you one-step closer to the Success you want and deserve. As Success Seekers, everything we do is an investment. Nothing we do is a sacrifice. Denying ourselves of anything that we currently want just so we can have the Success we know is down the road is an INVESTMENT. When you skip getting something you want now to reach your goals later, I want you to say this to yourself: **"Everything I do is an INVESTMENT. Nothing I do is a sacrifice. I am WINNING. I am Successful."**

How you view your actions and behaviors is just as important as how you act and behave. To reach your goals, to achieve the Success you have identified for yourself, you must first change how you see and think about things. Our perspective, our view of things is what sometimes keeps us from reaching our goals. It is so very important that you adjust your view of things to see yourself as Successful and WINNING in all that you do. Changing your mindset is an INVESTMENT in itself - probably the most important one you will ever make. It is an INVESTMENT in you.

# TIME ~~MANAGEMENT~~ MAXING

To get you started on this journey without discussing one of the most important resources that you have at your fingertips and how you should use it would be a disservice. That resource is *TIME*. We all have the same 24 hours in a day, the same 52 weeks in a year and the same 365 days in that year. We receive lots of advice about how we should manage our time and there are numerous strategies that will help us do it. When we are told how to manage our time, we are told to do things that are "constructive". Being "constructive" is important and doing so is probably a good use of our time and a good strategy for managing it. What is often overlooked is whether your "constructive" use of time is you maxing the use of your time. Maxing your time is you making the most of the time you have with your constructive activities and ensuring that those activities are **ALL** focused on achieving your goals. You can manage your time well, you can be constructive and yet none of your actions may be focused on you achieving your Success. When all of your actions and all of your time is focused on reaching your goals then you are *Time Maxing*. Time Maxing is your goal when it comes to your time. Simply managing your time is not enough. You should be so focused on achieving your goals that if you cannot see how an activity fits into you achieving your goals you replace that activity with another one that is linked to you reaching your Success. To be Successful do not simply manage your time, MAX IT.

In this journal, before you start your 66 days journey, you will spend time identifying the activities that will be included in your ideal morning and your ideal evening. This will ensure you are time maxing and being intentional about carving out time for your Success. I ask that you complete this task in pencil. We as young ladies and women know all too well, life changes constantly. Changes to this ideal day should be reserved for major changes. For example, you originally identify 5:30 a.m. as your time to journal, however, your spouse (who has handled the task of dropping your child off at school) has gotten a new job which requires you to assume the responsibility of dropping your child off. To do this, you will have to journal at 9:00 p.m. instead. This major change should be recorded. **Do note that it is important to stay as close to your ideal morning and evening as possible. You have made a commitment to yourself to make YOU a priority. So, PRIORITIZE YOU!**

# HOW TO USE THIS JOURNAL

Within these pages you will find quotes from various literary works, including the Holy Bible and other life and self-improvement teachings by famous and not so famous people, all of which I expect you to use for your elevation and for you to assist others with elevating themselves.

Let us begin with this Bible verse...in Galatians 5:22 God says, "But the fruit of the Spirit is love, joy, peace, longsuffering, gentleness, goodness, faith." I think it is important for us to address the underlined word in this statement before we go further. Without referencing Webster's Dictionary or the Internet, we know and understand that the word "*long*" means that something has a stretched out existence. And then, God says to us that this stretched out existence will be composed of *suffering*, which equates to *hardships*, *despair*, *trouble*, *uncomfortableness*, *work*, *tiredness*, *uneasiness*, *bad times* — things that you will be unhappy about and maybe even cause you mental and/or physical discomfort.

However, Jesus also said in John 10:10, "I have come that you may have life, and that you may have *it* more abundantly." Essentially, this statement tells us that it is our **Divine** right to live a good life, to enjoy life, to have as much as we would like from life. These two statements together tell us one thing; our Success **WILL NOT** come without some difficult times. *But*, if we will endure the difficult times, we will earn our Success, which is waiting for us at the other end.

To say it bluntly, difficult times are part of the process. You will have to stop at "failure" on your road to Success, but you do not have to stay there. For that reason, to help you navigate your way to your Success with the least number of failure stops along the way, I have developed this journal. To start, you will write down your life goals. This will be what YOU want most out of life. Emphasis is placed on "what YOU want most", not your parents, society, friends, co-workers, or anyone else. Your Success is about YOU. There will be six main categories for which you will record your life goals. These include: (1) your personal happiness, (2) your physical health/fitness, (3) your mental wellness, (4) your financial health/wellness, (5) your family/social, and (6) your career. Understand that there can be more than one goal per category. You can have two main goals or Two Plan A's, as I like to call them. You are not limited to what you can do or the Success you can have. But, you MUST plan for any Success you expect. After you complete this task, select one category to focus on for the next 66 days. (Don't worry, after the first 66 days, you can select another category and start the journey again, as many times as you like.) Next, write down the things that will help you reach these goals. These are your intermediate or midpoint goals. Your midpoint goals help you to realize small wins through your journey that will keep you Inspired. Third, write down the things that let you know you are making progress towards achieving your goals. You will measure your success by these three things. Afterwards, write down the investments you will make in yourself that will ensure you achieve the Success you want and deserve.

Wait! You're not done yet. To ensure you get what you want out of this journal you have to commit to writing in it each day. (If you miss a day, that is okay...JUST DO NOT MISS TWO DAYS IN A ROW.) You want to build a habit of writing down daily goals each day, tracking your Success towards achieving them, and reflecting on your progress in the evening—each evening. Once this process is part of your daily behaviors and becomes a habit for you, you will be much closer to your Success.

Here are examples that will help you as you fill in your daily activities and accomplishments.

*Life*

# GOALS

EXAMPLE

► Personal Happiness:

*Find one thing each day to be happy about.*

► Physical Health/Fitness:

*Lose 30 pounds in 60 days, Maintain the weight loss, and engage in cardio and strength training exercises at least 6 days per week.*

► Mental Wellness

*Manage my stress level and commitments while ensuring I make time for myself at least once per week.*

► Financial Health/Wellness

Obtain and maintain a 800 credit score, establish a savings account of $50k.

► Family/Social:

Have uninterrupted time with family at least twice per month, spending 30 minutes of quality time with my son each day, having an adventure with a friend monthly.

► Career:

Establish a business with a full-time role for myself which will lead to independent financial wealth while being a positive contributor to society.

# MY IDEAL MORNING/EVENING ROUTINE

| Morning | | Evening | |
|---|---|---|---|
| Wake up | 5:30 a.m. | 1:00 p.m. | Lunch |
| Hydrate with 8 oz. water | 5:35 a.m. | 2:00 p.m. | Hydrate with 8 oz. water |
| Pray/Journal | 5:40 a.m. | 5:00 p.m. | Pick up son |
| Prepare for the day | 6:00 a.m. | 5:05 p.m. | Hydrate with 8 oz. water |
| Drop son off | 7:30 a.m. | 6:00 p.m. | Spend time with family |
| Hydrate with 8 oz. water | 8:05 a.m. | 7:00 p.m. | Dinner |
| Take a walk | 9:00 a.m. | 8:00 p.m. | Hydrate with 8 oz. water |
| Hydrate with 8 oz. water | 9:25 a.m. | 9:00 p.m. | Shower |
| Take a walk | 11:00 a.m. | 10:00 p.m. | Read/Reflect/ Journal |
| Hydrate with 8 oz. water | 11:25 a.m. | 10:30 p.m. | Prepare for Bed |

# LET'S BEGIN!

### 1. Identify your **Two Plan A's**

Quite often when young people describe their goals to adults, those adults might respond by saying, "What is your plan b?" or "What is your fall back plan?" This type of thinking is absolutely WRONG. The problem with a plan b or a fall back plan is that once it is introduced to you and you decide to adopt these secondary plan concepts, you immediately accept the fact that you can fail. You immediately give life to the possibility that you will not achieve your goals. So right here and right now, I need you to decide that you will not have a plan b nor will you have a fall back plan. Do not accept failure. INSTEAD, why not have Two Plan A's?

Having Two Plan A's is very different from having a plan b or a fall back plan. Having Two Plan A's is you choosing to succeed in more than one thing. Everyone has more in them than they believe they do and certainly more than they are comfortable with doing. Everyone is interested in doing or being more than one thing. When you elect to have Two Plan A's you are deciding to be great at more than one thing.

You must take several steps before you can start to pursue your Success. The first step is to identify the goal you want to achieve. No one in the history of being Successful has ever achieved their Success without identifying a goal and an endpoint. Most of us have goals in mind or things we want to achieve in life. Sometimes we are not able to state our goals clearly and that is okay. To help with this, I have an exercise I want you to try.

## STEP 1

**Write out your biggest goal for your future.**

I call this your long-term goal. It will normally take some time before you reach this goal but it is very important for you to have. If you find it hard to write this out, think of it this way… if you could make a million dollars *doing whatever you wanted*, what would you do? Nothing that you can think of and no idea you might have is too silly here. Just write it down.

▶ My Biggest Goal for My Future is/is to:

Great! You have just completed the first step in achieving Success for yourself. Do not worry if your goal is not perfect. You can come back and make it better later. The next thing you will need to do is take the second step on this journey.

**STEP 2**

**Write down the top three things that you will first need to do to help you achieve your goal.**

These three things are what we like to call your short-term goals. If this is hard to understand think of it this way, if your main goal was to eat an entire pizza, you could not do it by placing the whole thing in your mouth at one time. You would have to eat slice one, slice two, slice three…until you had eaten the whole pizza. In this case, your main goal (*long-term goal*) is the entire pizza and each slice of the pizza is a *short-term goal* to help you get there. Now that you understand that, go ahead and write down the **top three things you need to do within the next year (12 months) to reach your long-term goal.** These three things could also be behaviors that you may need to change to help you reach your goal. It is always good to ask others who you respect to help you with this step. I suggest you talk to your parents, spouse, pastor, or even a trusted principal and honest friend. Trust me, they will certainly be impressed that you asked them to help you with this question and will probably be thrilled to give you good advice.

1.

_____

_____

2.

_____

_____

3.

_____

_____

Now that you have completed Step 2, you will need to make sure you can measure your Success.

**Write down at least three different ways you will be able to tell if you are on track to meeting your goals.**

Let me give you an example. If your long-term goal is to go to college, one way to measure your progress towards achieving your goal might be to graduate from high school. Another measure of your progress may be to apply for college or take the ACT exam. These are all things that will help you achieve your long-term goal of going to college. Write down three ways you will measure your progress.

1.

_____

_____

2.

_____

_____

3.

_____

_____

Please understand how important it is for you to establish ways for you to measure your Success. You need to know that you are you are doing well and making good progress in achieving your goals. This will help keep you inspired about the direction you are going in and provide you with more fuel for your forward movement.

Step 4 is even more important than Step 1. In this step, you take responsibility or increase your responsibility in achieving your Success. You must keep in mind that **your Success is your responsibility**... no one else's. Taking responsibility for your own Success will require you to do some things you may not already be doing. How you spend your time may be something you consider changing. Also, you may have to educate yourself about things you don't already know about. You will certainly need to find a mentor...more than one. Regardless of what anyone tells you, nobody has ever succeeded on his or her own. Those who are really Successful will more than likely tell you they had a mentor or someone who showed them the way. Mentors are very important to your Success.

## STEP 4

**Finish the following statements with your own answers.**

A. I will make time for my Success by:

B. I will increase my knowledge about:

C. I will ask the following people to advise/ mentor me:

_____

_____

_____

**Plan to Plan: Design your ideal daily routine.**

As mentioned earlier in this journal, as young ladies and women, we must plan to plan our wins. We must be intentional about our Success journey. While you may not be able to stick to this routine each day, it is important to get as close to it as possible. This will ensure you have the time carved out to reach your Success.

*Life*

# GOALS

► Personal Happiness:

► Physical Health/Fitness:

► Mental Wellness

► Financial Health/Wellness

► Family/Social:

► Career:

# MY IDEAL MORNING/EVENING ROUTINE

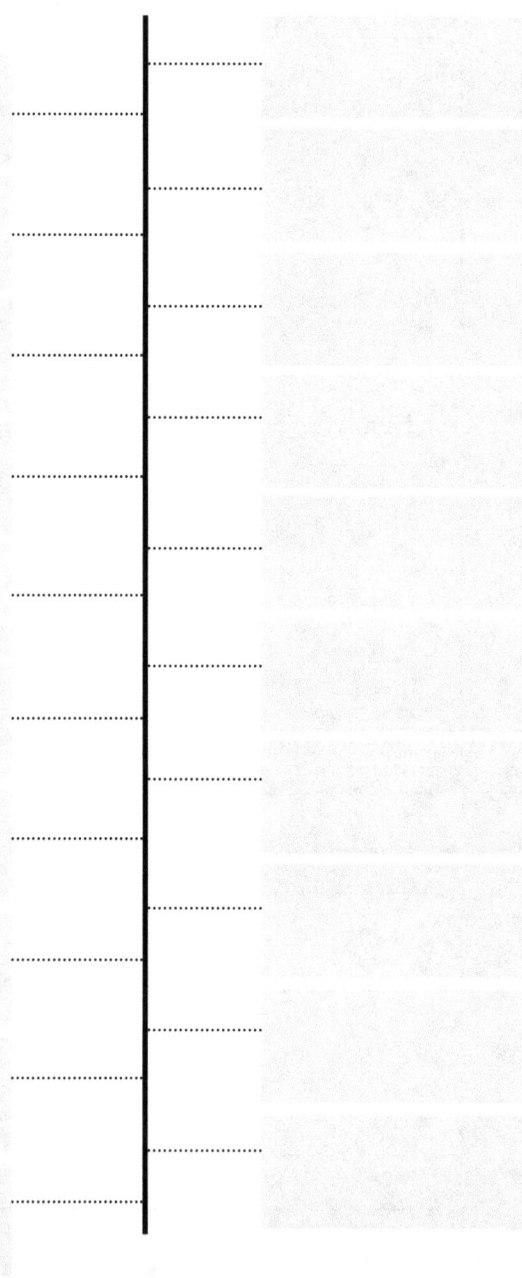

## 3 BOOKS TO READ FOR MOTIVATION

- ► *Grit: The Power of Passion and Perseverance* by Angela Duckworth

- ► *Girl, Wash Your Face: Stop Believing the Lies About Who You Are So You Can Become Who You Were Meant to Be* by Rachel Hollis

- ► *Be Unapologetically You: A Self Love Guide for Women of Color* by Adeline Bird

## DAY 1, Date:

*I make no apology for making myself my #1 priority. If I fail to take care of myself, I will have nothing to offer others.*

—**Dr. J.K. Ellis,** *Businesswoman & Investor*

## MORNING PLANNING

▶ I choose to have joy today because:

▶ I am working towards my goal because:

**My Plan A. is:**

► The **first** thing I will do today to get me closer to achieving my Plan A. is:

Start Time: _____     End Time: _____

► The **second** thing I will do today to get me closer to achieving my Plan A. is:

Start Time: _____     End Time: _____

**My next plan A is:**

_____

_____

► The **first** thing I will do today to get me closer to achieving my next Plan A is:

Start Time: _____ End Time: _____

► The **second** thing I will do today to get me closer to achieving my next Plan A is:

Start Time: _____ End Time: _____

► Today, I will talk with/communicate with Mr./Ms./Dr. _____ about:

## EVENING REFLECTION

► I made ME a priority today by:

► The single most important thing I did today to get me closer to my goals was:

► The one thing that hurt my progress the most today was:

► I will overcome this obstacle tomorrow by:

*Fear is the devil trying to keep you from your Success.*

—Dr. S.K. Ellis,
*Investor & Entrepreneur*

## MORNING PLANNING

▶  I choose to have joy today because:

▶  I am working towards my goal because:

## My Plan A. is:

► The **first** thing I will do today to get me closer to achieving my Plan A. is:

Start Time: _____     End Time: _____

► The **second** thing I will do today to get me closer to achieving my Plan A. is:

Start Time: _____     End Time: _____

## My next plan A is:

_____

_____

► The **first** thing I will do today to get me closer to achieving my next Plan A is:

Start Time: _____ End Time: _____

► The **second** thing I will do today to get me closer to achieving my next Plan A is:

Start Time: _____ End Time: _____

► Today, I will talk with/communicate with Mr./ Ms./Dr. _____ about:

## EVENING REFLECTION

► I made ME a priority today by:

► The single most important thing I did today to get me closer to my goals was:

► The one thing that hurt my progress the most today was:

► I will overcome this obstacle tomorrow by:

## DAY 3, Date:

*Fearlessness is like a muscle. I know from my own life that the more I exercise it the more natural it becomes to not let my fears run me.*

**—ARIANNA HUFFINGTON,**
*Author, Syndicated Columnist & Businesswoman*

## MORNING PLANNING

► I choose to have joy today because:

► I am working towards my goal because:

## My Plan A. is:

▶ The **first** thing I will do today to get me closer to achieving my Plan A. is:

Start Time: _____ End Time: _____

▶ The **second** thing I will do today to get me closer to achieving my Plan A. is:

Start Time: _____ End Time: _____

## My next plan A is:

_____

_____

► The **first** thing I will do today to get me closer to achieving my next Plan A is:

Start Time: _____     End Time: _____

► The **second** thing I will do today to get me closer to achieving my next Plan A is:

Start Time: _____     End Time: _____

► Today, I will talk with/communicate with Mr./ Ms./Dr. _____ about:

## EVENING REFLECTION

► I made ME a priority today by:

► The single most important thing I did today to get me closer to my goals was:

► The one thing that hurt my progress the most today was:

► I will overcome this obstacle tomorrow by:

## DAY 4, Date:

*To all the little girls who are watching, never doubt that you are valuable and powerful and deserving of every chance and opportunity in the world to pursue and achieve your own dreams.*

—**HILLARY CLINTON**,
*Former United States Secretary of State*

## MORNING PLANNING

► I choose to have joy today because:

► I am working towards my goal because:

**My Plan A. is:**

► The **first** thing I will do today to get me closer to achieving my Plan A. is:

Start Time: _____    End Time: _____

► The **second** thing I will do today to get me closer to achieving my Plan A. is:

Start Time: _____    End Time: _____

## My next plan A is:

_____

_____

► The **first** thing I will do today to get me closer to achieving my next Plan A is:

Start Time: _____    End Time: _____

► The **second** thing I will do today to get me closer to achieving my next Plan A is:

Start Time: _____    End Time: _____

► Today, I will talk with/communicate with Mr./Ms./Dr. _____ about:

## EVENING REFLECTION

► I made ME a priority today by:

► The single most important thing I did today to get me closer to my goals was:

► The one thing that hurt my progress the most today was:

► I will overcome this obstacle tomorrow by:

## DAY 5, Date:

*The first act of courage is to acknowledge that you are afraid. The second is to act anyway.*

—**DR. S.K. ELLIS,** *Investor & Entrepreneur*

## MORNING PLANNING

▶ I choose to have joy today because:

▶ I am working towards my goal because:

## My Plan A. is:

► The **first** thing I will do today to get me closer to achieving my Plan A. is:

Start Time: _____ End Time: _____

► The **second** thing I will do today to get me closer to achieving my Plan A. is:

Start Time: _____ End Time: _____

## My next plan A is:

_____

_____

► The **first** thing I will do today to get me closer to achieving my next Plan A is:

Start Time: _____    End Time: _____

► The **second** thing I will do today to get me closer to achieving my next Plan A is:

Start Time: _____    End Time: _____

► Today, I will talk with/communicate with Mr./ Ms./Dr. _____ about:

## EVENING REFLECTION

► I made ME a priority today by:

► The single most important thing I did today to get me closer to my goals was:

► The one thing that hurt my progress the most today was:

► I will overcome this obstacle tomorrow by:

## 5-DAY ACCOUNTABILITY CHECK

*During the past 5 days...*

► I made time for my success by:

► I increased my knowledge about:

► I asked for advice/guidance from:

_____

_____

_____

► Over the next 5 days I will talk with/communicate with Mr./Ms./Dr. _____ about:

*Dream with ambition, lead with conviction, and see yourself in a way that others might not see you, simply because they've never seen it before.*

—**KAMALA HARRIS,**
*Vice President of the United States of America*

## MORNING PLANNING

► I choose to have joy today because:

► I am working towards my goal because:

**My Plan A. is:**

► The **first** thing I will do today to get me closer to achieving my Plan A. is:

Start Time: _____  End Time: _____

► The **second** thing I will do today to get me closer to achieving my Plan A. is:

Start Time: _____  End Time: _____

## My next plan A is:

_____

_____

► The **first** thing I will do today to get me closer to achieving my next Plan A is:

Start Time: _____     End Time: _____

► The **second** thing I will do today to get me closer to achieving my next Plan A is:

Start Time: _____     End Time: _____

► Today, I will talk with/communicate with Mr./ Ms./Dr. _____ about:

## EVENING REFLECTION

► I made ME a priority today by:

► The single most important thing I did today to get me closer to my goals was:

► The one thing that hurt my progress the most today was:

► I will overcome this obstacle tomorrow by:

## DAY 7, Date:

*There are 5 D's to Success. Be Definite. Be Deliberate. Be Diligent. Be Determined. Be Damned if you do not win.*

—DR. S.K. ELLIS, *Investor & Entrepreneur*

## MORNING PLANNING

► I choose to have joy today because:

► I am working towards my goal because:

## My Plan A. is:

► The **first** thing I will do today to get me closer to achieving my Plan A. is:

Start Time: _____ End Time: _____

► The **second** thing I will do today to get me closer to achieving my Plan A. is:

Start Time: _____ End Time: _____

## My next plan A is:

_____

_____

► The **first** thing I will do today to get me closer to achieving my next Plan A is:

Start Time: _____     End Time: _____

► The **second** thing I will do today to get me closer to achieving my next Plan A is:

Start Time: _____     End Time: _____

► Today, I will talk with/communicate with Mr./Ms./Dr. _____ about:

## EVENING REFLECTION

► I made ME a priority today by:

► The single most important thing I did today to get me closer to my goals was:

► The one thing that hurt my progress the most today was:

► I will overcome this obstacle tomorrow by:

## DAY 8, Date:

*The woman I was yesterday, introduced me to the woman I am today; which makes me very excited about meeting the woman I will become tomorrow.*

—POETIC EVOLUTION, *Author*

## MORNING PLANNING

► I choose to have joy today because:

► I am working towards my goal because:

## My Plan A. is:

► The **first** thing I will do today to get me closer to achieving my Plan A. is:

Start Time: _____     End Time: _____

► The **second** thing I will do today to get me closer to achieving my Plan A. is:

Start Time: _____     End Time: _____

## My next plan A is:

_____

_____

► The **first** thing I will do today to get me closer to achieving my next Plan A is:

Start Time: _____ End Time: _____

► The **second** thing I will do today to get me closer to achieving my next Plan A is:

Start Time: _____ End Time: _____

► Today, I will talk with/communicate with Mr./Ms./Dr. _____ about:

## EVENING REFLECTION

► I made ME a priority today by:

► The single most important thing I did today to get me closer to my goals was:

► The one thing that hurt my progress the most today was:

► I will overcome this obstacle tomorrow by:

## DAY 9, Date:

*I never lose. I either win or learn.*

—**NELSON MANDELA,**
*Former President of South Africa*

## MORNING PLANNING

▶ I choose to have joy today because:

▶ I am working towards my goal because:

## My Plan A. is:

► The **first** thing I will do today to get me closer to achieving my Plan A. is:

Start Time: _____ End Time: _____

► The **second** thing I will do today to get me closer to achieving my Plan A. is:

Start Time: _____ End Time: _____

## My next plan A is:

_____

_____

► The **first** thing I will do today to get me closer to achieving my next Plan A is:

Start Time: _____ End Time: _____

► The **second** thing I will do today to get me closer to achieving my next Plan A is:

Start Time: _____ End Time: _____

► Today, I will talk with/communicate with Mr./ Ms./Dr. _____ about:

## EVENING REFLECTION

▶ I made ME a priority today by:

▶ The single most important thing I did today to get me closer to my goals was:

▶ The one thing that hurt my progress the most today was:

▶ I will overcome this obstacle tomorrow by:

## DAY 10, Date:

*Success, they taught me, is built on the foundation of courage, hard-work and individual responsibility. Despite what some would have us believe, success is not built on resentment and fears.*

—SUSANA MARTINEZ,
*Former Governor of New Mexico*

## MORNING PLANNING

► I choose to have joy today because:

► I am working towards my goal because:

## My Plan A. is:

► The **first** thing I will do today to get me closer to achieving my Plan A. is:

Start Time: _____    End Time: _____

► The **second** thing I will do today to get me closer to achieving my Plan A. is:

Start Time: _____    End Time: _____

## My next plan A is:

_____

_____

► The **first** thing I will do today to get me closer to achieving my next Plan A is:

Start Time: _____     End Time: _____

► The **second** thing I will do today to get me closer to achieving my next Plan A is:

Start Time: _____     End Time: _____

► Today, I will talk with/communicate with Mr./Ms./Dr. _____ about:

## EVENING REFLECTION

► I made ME a priority today by:

► The single most important thing I did today to get me closer to my goals was:

► The one thing that hurt my progress the most today was:

► I will overcome this obstacle tomorrow by:

## 5-DAY ACCOUNTABILITY CHECK

*During the past 5 days...*

► I made time for my success by:

► I increased my knowledge about:

► I asked for advice/guidance from:

_____

_____

_____

► Over the next 5 days I will talk with/communicate with Mr./Ms./Dr. _____ about:

## DAY 11, Date:

*Don't dream of winning, train for it.*

**—MO FARAH,**
*British Long-Distance Runner*

## MORNING PLANNING

▶ I choose to have joy today because:

▶ I am working towards my goal because:

## My Plan A. is:

_____

_____

► The **first** thing I will do today to get me closer to achieving my Plan A. is:

Start Time: _____ End Time: _____

► The **second** thing I will do today to get me closer to achieving my Plan A. is:

Start Time: _____ End Time: _____

## My next plan A is:

_____

_____

► The **first** thing I will do today to get me closer to achieving my next Plan A is:

Start Time: _____ End Time: _____

► The **second** thing I will do today to get me closer to achieving my next Plan A is:

Start Time: _____ End Time: _____

► Today, I will talk with/communicate with Mr./Ms./Dr. _____ about:

## EVENING REFLECTION

► I made ME a priority today by:

► The single most important thing I did today to get me closer to my goals was:

► The one thing that hurt my progress the most today was:

► I will overcome this obstacle tomorrow by:

*It's not selfish to love yourself, take care of yourself, and make your happiness a priority. It's necessary.*

—**MANDY HALE,**
*Author*

## MORNING PLANNING

► I choose to have joy today because:

► I am working towards my goal because:

**My Plan A. is:**

► The **first** thing I will do today to get me closer to achieving my Plan A. is:

Start Time: _____     End Time: _____

► The **second** thing I will do today to get me closer to achieving my Plan A. is:

Start Time: _____     End Time: _____

## My next plan A is:

_____

_____

► The **first** thing I will do today to get me closer to achieving my next Plan A is:

Start Time: _____ End Time: _____

► The **second** thing I will do today to get me closer to achieving my next Plan A is:

Start Time: _____ End Time: _____

► Today, I will talk with/communicate with Mr./ Ms./Dr. _____ about:

## EVENING REFLECTION

► I made ME a priority today by:

► The single most important thing I did today to get me closer to my goals was:

► The one thing that hurt my progress the most today was:

► I will overcome this obstacle tomorrow by:

*Believe and act as if it were impossible to fail.*

—CHARLES KETTERING,
*American Inventor*

## MORNING PLANNING

▶ I choose to have joy today because:

▶ I am working towards my goal because:

**My Plan A. is:**

► The **first** thing I will do today to get me closer to achieving my Plan A. is:

Start Time: _____     End Time: _____

► The **second** thing I will do today to get me closer to achieving my Plan A. is:

Start Time: _____     End Time: _____

## My next plan A is:

_____

_____

► The **first** thing I will do today to get me closer to achieving my next Plan A is:

Start Time: _____    End Time: _____

► The **second** thing I will do today to get me closer to achieving my next Plan A is:

Start Time: _____    End Time: _____

► Today, I will talk with/communicate with Mr./Ms./Dr. _____ about:

## EVENING REFLECTION

► I made ME a priority today by:

► The single most important thing I did today to get me closer to my goals was:

► The one thing that hurt my progress the most today was:

► I will overcome this obstacle tomorrow by:

## DAY 14, Date:

*The best revenge is massive Success.*

—**FRANK SINATRA**, *Actor*

## MORNING PLANNING

► I choose to have joy today because:

► I am working towards my goal because:

## My Plan A. is:

_____

_____

► The **first** thing I will do today to get me closer to achieving my Plan A. is:

Start Time: _____ End Time: _____

► The **second** thing I will do today to get me closer to achieving my Plan A. is:

Start Time: _____ End Time: _____

## My next plan A is:

_____

_____

► The **first** thing I will do today to get me closer to achieving my next Plan A is:

Start Time: _____ End Time: _____

► The **second** thing I will do today to get me closer to achieving my next Plan A is:

Start Time: _____ End Time: _____

► Today, I will talk with/communicate with Mr./Ms./Dr. _____ about:

## EVENING REFLECTION

► I made ME a priority today by:

► The single most important thing I did today to get me closer to my goals was:

► The one thing that hurt my progress the most today was:

► I will overcome this obstacle tomorrow by:

*I've grown most not from victories, but setbacks. If winning is God's reward, then losing is how He teaches us.*

—**SERENA WILLIAMS,** *American Tennis Player*

## MORNING PLANNING

► I choose to have joy today because:

► I am working towards my goal because:

**My Plan A. is:**

► The **first** thing I will do today to get me closer to achieving my Plan A. is:

Start Time: _____     End Time: _____

► The **second** thing I will do today to get me closer to achieving my Plan A. is:

Start Time: _____     End Time: _____

## My next plan A is:

_____

_____

► The **first** thing I will do today to get me closer to achieving my next Plan A is:

Start Time: _____ End Time: _____

► The **second** thing I will do today to get me closer to achieving my next Plan A is:

Start Time: _____ End Time: _____

► Today, I will talk with/communicate with Mr./Ms./Dr. _____ about:

## EVENING REFLECTION

► I made ME a priority today by:

► The single most important thing I did today to get me closer to my goals was:

► The one thing that hurt my progress the most today was:

► I will overcome this obstacle tomorrow by:

## 5-DAY ACCOUNTABILITY CHECK

*During the past 5 days...*

▶ I made time for my success by:

▶ I increased my knowledge about:

▶ I asked for advice/guidance from:

▶ Over the next 5 days I will talk with/communicate with Mr./Ms./Dr. _____ about:

*I knew well that the only way I could get that door open was to knock it down; because I knocked all of them down.*

—SADIE TANNER MOSSELL ALEXANDER,
*American Solicitor*

## MORNING PLANNING

► I choose to have joy today because:

► I am working towards my goal because:

**My Plan A. is:**

► The **first** thing I will do today to get me closer to achieving my Plan A. is:

Start Time: _____    End Time: _____

► The **second** thing I will do today to get me closer to achieving my Plan A. is:

Start Time: _____    End Time: _____

## My next plan A is:

_____

_____

► The **first** thing I will do today to get me closer to achieving my next Plan A is:

Start Time: _____     End Time: _____

► The **second** thing I will do today to get me closer to achieving my next Plan A is:

Start Time: _____     End Time: _____

► Today, I will talk with/communicate with Mr./ Ms./Dr. _____ about:

## EVENING REFLECTION

► I made ME a priority today by:

► The single most important thing I did today to get me closer to my goals was:

► The one thing that hurt my progress the most today was:

► I will overcome this obstacle tomorrow by:

*"Do or do not. There is no try."*

—**YODA**, *Jedi Master*

## MORNING PLANNING

► I choose to have joy today because:

► I am working towards my goal because:

## My Plan A. is:

► The **first** thing I will do today to get me closer to achieving my Plan A. is:

Start Time: _____     End Time: _____

► The **second** thing I will do today to get me closer to achieving my Plan A. is:

Start Time: _____     End Time: _____

## My next plan A is:

_____

_____

► The **first** thing I will do today to get me closer to achieving my next Plan A is:

Start Time: _____    End Time: _____

► The **second** thing I will do today to get me closer to achieving my next Plan A is:

Start Time: _____    End Time: _____

► Today, I will talk with/communicate with Mr./ Ms./Dr. _____ about:

## EVENING REFLECTION

► I made ME a priority today by:

> [blank box]

► The single most important thing I did today to get me closer to my goals was:

> [blank box]

► The one thing that hurt my progress the most today was:

> [blank box]

► I will overcome this obstacle tomorrow by:

> [blank box]

DAY 18, Date:

*There are two powers in the world, one is the sword and other is the pen. There is a third power stronger than both; that of woman.*

—**MALALA YOUSAFZAI,** *Pakistani Activist*

## MORNING PLANNING

► I choose to have joy today because:

► I am working towards my goal because:

**My Plan A. is:**

► The **first** thing I will do today to get me closer to achieving my Plan A. is:

Start Time: _____ End Time: _____

► The **second** thing I will do today to get me closer to achieving my Plan A. is:

Start Time: _____ End Time: _____

## My next plan A is:

_____

_____

▶ The **first** thing I will do today to get me closer to achieving my next Plan A is:

Start Time: _____ End Time: _____

▶ The **second** thing I will do today to get me closer to achieving my next Plan A is:

Start Time: _____ End Time: _____

▶ Today, I will talk with/communicate with Mr./Ms./Dr. _____ about:

## EVENING REFLECTION

► I made ME a priority today by:

► The single most important thing I did today to get me closer to my goals was:

► The one thing that hurt my progress the most today was:

► I will overcome this obstacle tomorrow by:

## DAY 19, Date:

*Success is not a destination. Failure is not an event. Success is a process, failure is a choice.*

—**DJ BENEDICT,** *Musical Artist*

## MORNING PLANNING

► I choose to have joy today because:

► I am working towards my goal because:

## My Plan A. is:

► The **first** thing I will do today to get me closer to achieving my Plan A. is:

Start Time: _____ End Time: _____

► The **second** thing I will do today to get me closer to achieving my Plan A. is:

Start Time: _____ End Time: _____

## My next plan A is:

_____

_____

► The **first** thing I will do today to get me closer to achieving my next Plan A is:

Start Time: _____ End Time: _____

► The **second** thing I will do today to get me closer to achieving my next Plan A is:

Start Time: _____ End Time: _____

► Today, I will talk with/communicate with Mr./ Ms./Dr. _____ about:

## EVENING REFLECTION

► I made ME a priority today by:

► The single most important thing I did today to get me closer to my goals was:

► The one thing that hurt my progress the most today was:

► I will overcome this obstacle tomorrow by:

## DAY 20, Date:

*There is nothing stronger than a broken woman who has rebuilt herself.*

**—Hannah Gadsby,**
*Australian Comedian*

## MORNING PLANNING

▶ I choose to have joy today because:

▶ I am working towards my goal because:

**My Plan A. is:**

► The **first** thing I will do today to get me closer to achieving my Plan A. is:

Start Time: _____     End Time: _____

► The **second** thing I will do today to get me closer to achieving my Plan A. is:

Start Time: _____     End Time: _____

## My next plan A is:

_____

_____

► The **first** thing I will do today to get me closer to achieving my next Plan A is:

Start Time: _____    End Time: _____

► The **second** thing I will do today to get me closer to achieving my next Plan A is:

Start Time: _____    End Time: _____

► Today, I will talk with/communicate with Mr./ Ms./Dr. _____ about:

## EVENING REFLECTION

▶ I made ME a priority today by:

▶ The single most important thing I did today to get me closer to my goals was:

▶ The one thing that hurt my progress the most today was:

▶ I will overcome this obstacle tomorrow by:

## 5-DAY ACCOUNTABILITY CHECK

*During the past 5 days...*

▶ I made time for my success by:

▶ I increased my knowledge about:

▶ I asked for advice/guidance from:

_____

_____

_____

▶ Over the next 5 days I will talk with/communicate with Mr./Ms./Dr. _____ about:

## 3 BOOKS TO INSPIRE YOU

► *Becoming* by Michelle Obama

► *SOAR* by T.D. Jakes

► *Daring Greatly: How the Courage to Be Vulnerable Transforms the Way We Live, Love, Parent, and Lead* by Brené Brown

*God is within her, she will not fail; God will help her at break of day.*

—PSALMS 46:5

## MORNING PLANNING

▶ I choose to have joy today because:

▶ I am working towards my goal because:

## My Plan A. is:

► The **first** thing I will do today to get me closer to achieving my Plan A. is:

Start Time: _____     End Time: _____

► The **second** thing I will do today to get me closer to achieving my Plan A. is:

Start Time: _____     End Time: _____

## My next plan A is:

_____

_____

► The **first** thing I will do today to get me closer to achieving my next Plan A is:

Start Time: _____ End Time: _____

► The **second** thing I will do today to get me closer to achieving my next Plan A is:

Start Time: _____ End Time: _____

► Today, I will talk with/communicate with Mr./Ms./Dr. _____ about:

## EVENING REFLECTION

► I made ME a priority today by:

► The single most important thing I did today to get me closer to my goals was:

► The one thing that hurt my progress the most today was:

► I will overcome this obstacle tomorrow by:

*Whatever you fear most has no power—it is your fear that has the power.*

**—OPRAH WINFREY,**
*Television Producer, Actress, Author,*
*Philanthropist, Host*

## MORNING PLANNING

► I choose to have joy today because:

► I am working towards my goal because:

**My Plan A. is:**

► The **first** thing I will do today to get me closer to achieving my Plan A. is:

Start Time: _____ End Time: _____

► The **second** thing I will do today to get me closer to achieving my Plan A. is:

Start Time: _____ End Time: _____

## My next plan A is:

_____

_____

► The **first** thing I will do today to get me closer to achieving my next Plan A is:

Start Time: _____     End Time: _____

► The **second** thing I will do today to get me closer to achieving my next Plan A is:

Start Time: _____     End Time: _____

► Today, I will talk with/communicate with Mr./ Ms./Dr. _____ about:

## EVENING REFLECTION

► I made ME a priority today by:

► The single most important thing I did today to get me closer to my goals was:

► The one thing that hurt my progress the most today was:

► I will overcome this obstacle tomorrow by:

*Blessed is she who has believed that the Lord would fulfill His promises to her!*

—LUKE 1:45

## MORNING PLANNING

▶ I choose to have joy today because:

▶ I am working towards my goal because:

**My Plan A. is:**

► The **first** thing I will do today to get me closer to achieving my Plan A. is:

Start Time: _____ End Time: _____

► The **second** thing I will do today to get me closer to achieving my Plan A. is:

Start Time: _____ End Time: _____

## My next plan A is:

_____

_____

► The **first** thing I will do today to get me closer to achieving my next Plan A is:

Start Time: _____ End Time: _____

► The **second** thing I will do today to get me closer to achieving my next Plan A is:

Start Time: _____ End Time: _____

► Today, I will talk with/communicate with Mr./Ms./Dr. _____ about:

## EVENING REFLECTION

▶ I made ME a priority today by:

[ ]

▶ The single most important thing I did today to get me closer to my goals was:

[ ]

▶ The one thing that hurt my progress the most today was:

[ ]

▶ I will overcome this obstacle tomorrow by:

[ ]

## DAY 24, Date:

*But remember the LORD your God, for it is He who gives you the ability to produce wealth, and so confirms His covenant, which He swore to your ancestors, as it is today.*

**—DEUTERONOMY 8:18**

## MORNING PLANNING

► I choose to have joy today because:

► I am working towards my goal because:

## My Plan A. is:

► The **first** thing I will do today to get me closer to achieving my Plan A. is:

Start Time: _____     End Time: _____

► The **second** thing I will do today to get me closer to achieving my Plan A. is:

Start Time: _____     End Time: _____

## My next plan A is:

_____

_____

► The **first** thing I will do today to get me closer to achieving my next Plan A is:

Start Time: _____ End Time: _____

► The **second** thing I will do today to get me closer to achieving my next Plan A is:

Start Time: _____ End Time: _____

► Today, I will talk with/communicate with Mr./Ms./Dr. _____ about:

## EVENING REFLECTION

► I made ME a priority today by:

► The single most important thing I did today to get me closer to my goals was:

► The one thing that hurt my progress the most today was:

► I will overcome this obstacle tomorrow by:

## DAY 25, Date:

*The generous soul will be made rich, and he who waters will also be watered himself.*

—**PROVERBS 11:25**

## MORNING PLANNING

► I choose to have joy today because:

► I am working towards my goal because:

## My Plan A. is:

► The **first** thing I will do today to get me closer to achieving my Plan A. is:

Start Time: _____ End Time: _____

► The **second** thing I will do today to get me closer to achieving my Plan A. is:

Start Time: _____ End Time: _____

## My next plan A is:

_____

_____

► The **first** thing I will do today to get me closer to achieving my next Plan A is:

Start Time: _____     End Time: _____

► The **second** thing I will do today to get me closer to achieving my next Plan A is:

Start Time: _____     End Time: _____

► Today, I will talk with/communicate with Mr./Ms./Dr. _____ about:

## EVENING REFLECTION

► I made ME a priority today by:

► The single most important thing I did today to get me closer to my goals was:

► The one thing that hurt my progress the most today was:

► I will overcome this obstacle tomorrow by:

## 5-DAY ACCOUNTABILITY CHECK

*During the past 5 days...*

► I made time for my success by:

► I increased my knowledge about:

► I asked for advice/guidance from:

_____

_____

_____

► Over the next 5 days I will talk with/communicate with Mr./Ms./Dr. _____ about:

## DAY 26, Date:

*Do the thing you think you cannot do.*

— **ELEANOR ROOSEVELT,**
*Former First Lady of the United States*

## MORNING PLANNING

▶ I choose to have joy today because:

▶ I am working towards my goal because:

## My Plan A. is:

► The **first** thing I will do today to get me closer to achieving my Plan A. is:

Start Time: _____ End Time: _____

► The **second** thing I will do today to get me closer to achieving my Plan A. is:

Start Time: _____ End Time: _____

## My next plan A is:

_____

_____

► The **first** thing I will do today to get me closer to achieving my next Plan A is:

Start Time: _____    End Time: _____

► The **second** thing I will do today to get me closer to achieving my next Plan A is:

Start Time: _____    End Time: _____

► Today, I will talk with/communicate with Mr./ Ms./Dr. _____ about:

## EVENING REFLECTION

► I made ME a priority today by:

► The single most important thing I did today to get me closer to my goals was:

► The one thing that hurt my progress the most today was:

► I will overcome this obstacle tomorrow by:

*Without leaps of imagination or dreaming, we lose the excitement of possibilities. Dreaming, after all, is a form of planning.*

—GLORIA STEINEM,
*American Feminist Journalist & Political Activists*

## MORNING PLANNING

▶ I choose to have joy today because:

▶ I am working towards my goal because:

**My Plan A. is:**

► The **first** thing I will do today to get me closer to achieving my Plan A. is:

Start Time: _____  End Time: _____

► The **second** thing I will do today to get me closer to achieving my Plan A. is:

Start Time: _____  End Time: _____

**My next plan A is:**

_____

_____

► The **first** thing I will do today to get me closer to achieving my next Plan A is:

Start Time: _____ End Time: _____

► The **second** thing I will do today to get me closer to achieving my next Plan A is:

Start Time: _____ End Time: _____

► Today, I will talk with/communicate with Mr./Ms./Dr. _____ about:

## EVENING REFLECTION

► I made ME a priority today by:

► The single most important thing I did today to get me closer to my goals was:

► The one thing that hurt my progress the most today was:

► I will overcome this obstacle tomorrow by:

**DAY 28, Date:**

*Success isn't about how much money you make.
It's about the difference you make in people's lives.*

—**MICHELLE OBAMA,**
*Former First Lady of the United States of America*

## MORNING PLANNING

► I choose to have joy today because:

► I am working towards my goal because:

## My Plan A. is:

► The **first** thing I will do today to get me closer to achieving my Plan A. is:

Start Time: _____ End Time: _____

► The **second** thing I will do today to get me closer to achieving my Plan A. is:

Start Time: _____ End Time: _____

## My next plan A is:

_____

_____

▶ The **first** thing I will do today to get me closer to achieving my next Plan A is:

Start Time: _____ End Time: _____

▶ The **second** thing I will do today to get me closer to achieving my next Plan A is:

Start Time: _____ End Time: _____

▶ Today, I will talk with/communicate with Mr./Ms./Dr. _____ about:

## EVENING REFLECTION

► I made ME a priority today by:

► The single most important thing I did today to get me closer to my goals was:

► The one thing that hurt my progress the most today was:

► I will overcome this obstacle tomorrow by:

**DAY 29, Date:**

*Success doesn't come to you; you've got to go to it.*
— **MARVA COLLINS,** *American Educator*

## MORNING PLANNING

► I choose to have joy today because:

► I am working towards my goal because:

**My Plan A. is:**

► The **first** thing I will do today to get me closer to achieving my Plan A. is:

Start Time: _____    End Time: _____

► The **second** thing I will do today to get me closer to achieving my Plan A. is:

Start Time: _____    End Time: _____

## My next plan A is:

_____

_____

▶ The **first** thing I will do today to get me closer to achieving my next Plan A is:

Start Time: _____ End Time: _____

▶ The **second** thing I will do today to get me closer to achieving my next Plan A is:

Start Time: _____ End Time: _____

▶ Today, I will talk with/communicate with Mr./Ms./Dr. _____ about:

## EVENING REFLECTION

► I made ME a priority today by:

► The single most important thing I did today to get me closer to my goals was:

► The one thing that hurt my progress the most today was:

► I will overcome this obstacle tomorrow by:

## DAY 30, Date:

*I never dreamed about Success. I worked for it.*

**—Estée Lauder,**
*American Businesswoman*

## MORNING PLANNING

► I choose to have joy today because:

► I am working towards my goal because:

## My Plan A. is:

► The **first** thing I will do today to get me closer to achieving my Plan A. is:

Start Time: _____ End Time: _____

► The **second** thing I will do today to get me closer to achieving my Plan A. is:

Start Time: _____ End Time: _____

## My next plan A is:

_____

_____

► The **first** thing I will do today to get me closer to achieving my next Plan A is:

Start Time: _____     End Time: _____

► The **second** thing I will do today to get me closer to achieving my next Plan A is:

Start Time: _____     End Time: _____

► Today, I will talk with/communicate with Mr./ Ms./Dr. _____ about:

## EVENING REFLECTION

► I made ME a priority today by:

►  The single most important thing I did today to get me closer to my goals was:

►  The one thing that hurt my progress the most today was:

►  I will overcome this obstacle tomorrow by:

## 5-DAY ACCOUNTABILITY CHECK

*During the past 5 days...*

► I made time for my success by:

► I increased my knowledge about:

► I asked for advice/guidance from:

_____

_____

_____

► Over the next 5 days I will talk with/communicate with Mr./Ms./Dr. _____ about:

*The soul of a lazy man desires, and has nothing; but the soul of the diligent shall be made rich.*

—**PROVERBS 13:4**

## MORNING PLANNING

► I choose to have joy today because:

► I am working towards my goal because:

**My Plan A. is:**

► The **first** thing I will do today to get me closer to achieving my Plan A. is:

Start Time: _____     End Time: _____

► The **second** thing I will do today to get me closer to achieving my Plan A. is:

Start Time: _____     End Time: _____

## My next plan A is:

_____

_____

► The **first** thing I will do today to get me closer to achieving my next Plan A is:

Start Time: _____ End Time: _____

► The **second** thing I will do today to get me closer to achieving my next Plan A is:

Start Time: _____ End Time: _____

► Today, I will talk with/communicate with Mr./Ms./Dr. _____ about:

## EVENING REFLECTION

▶ I made ME a priority today by:

▶ The single most important thing I did today to get me closer to my goals was:

▶ The one thing that hurt my progress the most today was:

▶ I will overcome this obstacle tomorrow by:

*Beloved, I pray that you may prosper in all things and be in health, just as your soul prospers.*

—3 JOHN 1:2

## MORNING PLANNING

► I choose to have joy today because:

► I am working towards my goal because:

**My Plan A. is:**

► The **first** thing I will do today to get me closer to achieving my Plan A. is:

Start Time: _____    End Time: _____

► The **second** thing I will do today to get me closer to achieving my Plan A. is:

Start Time: _____    End Time: _____

## My next plan A is:

_____

_____

► The **first** thing I will do today to get me closer to achieving my next Plan A is:

Start Time: _____ End Time: _____

► The **second** thing I will do today to get me closer to achieving my next Plan A is:

Start Time: _____ End Time: _____

► Today, I will talk with/communicate with Mr./Ms./Dr. _____ about:

## EVENING REFLECTION

► I made ME a priority today by:

► The single most important thing I did today to get me closer to my goals was:

► The one thing that hurt my progress the most today was:

► I will overcome this obstacle tomorrow by:

*Sí se puede! (Yes we can!).*

**—DOLORES HUERTA,**
*American Labor Leader & Civil Rights Activist*

## MORNING PLANNING

▶ I choose to have joy today because:

▶ I am working towards my goal because:

**My Plan A. is:**

► The **first** thing I will do today to get me closer to achieving my Plan A. is:

Start Time: _____    End Time: _____

► The **second** thing I will do today to get me closer to achieving my Plan A. is:

Start Time: _____    End Time: _____

## My next plan A is:

_____

_____

► The **first** thing I will do today to get me closer to achieving my next Plan A is:

Start Time: _____ End Time: _____

► The **second** thing I will do today to get me closer to achieving my next Plan A is:

Start Time: _____ End Time: _____

► Today, I will talk with/communicate with Mr./Ms./Dr. _____ about:

## EVENING REFLECTION

► I made ME a priority today by:

► The single most important thing I did today to get me closer to my goals was:

► The one thing that hurt my progress the most today was:

► I will overcome this obstacle tomorrow by:

*A woman with a voice is, by definition, a strong woman.*

— MELINDA GATES,
*American Philanthropist & Former*
*General Manager at Microsoft*

## MORNING PLANNING

▶ I choose to have joy today because:

▶ I am working towards my goal because:

## My Plan A. is:

► The **first** thing I will do today to get me closer to achieving my Plan A. is:

Start Time: _____ End Time: _____

► The **second** thing I will do today to get me closer to achieving my Plan A. is:

Start Time: _____ End Time: _____

## My next plan A is:

_____

_____

► The **first** thing I will do today to get me closer to achieving my next Plan A is:

Start Time: _____ End Time: _____

► The **second** thing I will do today to get me closer to achieving my next Plan A is:

Start Time: _____ End Time: _____

► Today, I will talk with/communicate with Mr./Ms./Dr. _____ about:

## EVENING REFLECTION

► I made ME a priority today by:

►  The single most important thing I did today to get
   me closer to my goals was:

►  The one thing that hurt my progress the most
   today was:

►  I will overcome this obstacle tomorrow by:

*Be like a diamond, precious and rare, not like a stone, found everywhere.*

—ANONYMOUS

## MORNING PLANNING

▶ I choose to have joy today because:

▶ I am working towards my goal because:

**My Plan A. is:**

► The **first** thing I will do today to get me closer to achieving my Plan A. is:

Start Time: _____     End Time: _____

► The **second** thing I will do today to get me closer to achieving my Plan A. is:

Start Time: _____     End Time: _____

## My next plan A is:

_____

_____

► The **first** thing I will do today to get me closer to achieving my next Plan A is:

Start Time: _____ End Time: _____

► The **second** thing I will do today to get me closer to achieving my next Plan A is:

Start Time: _____ End Time: _____

► Today, I will talk with/communicate with Mr./Ms./Dr. _____ about:

## EVENING REFLECTION

▶ I made ME a priority today by:

▶ The single most important thing I did today to get me closer to my goals was:

▶ The one thing that hurt my progress the most today was:

▶ I will overcome this obstacle tomorrow by:

## 5-DAY ACCOUNTABILITY CHECK

*During the past 5 days...*

▶ I made time for my success by:

▶ I increased my knowledge about:

▶ I asked for advice/guidance from:

_____

_____

_____

▶ Over the next 5 days I will talk with/communicate
with Mr./Ms./Dr. _____ about:

*Success means having the courage, the determination, and the will to become the person you believe you were meant to be.*

— **GEORGE SHEEHAN,** *Physician & Author*

## MORNING PLANNING

▶ I choose to have joy today because:

▶ I am working towards my goal because:

**My Plan A. is:**

► The **first** thing I will do today to get me closer to achieving my Plan A. is:

Start Time: _____ End Time: _____

► The **second** thing I will do today to get me closer to achieving my Plan A. is:

Start Time: _____ End Time: _____

## My next plan A is:

_____

_____

► The **first** thing I will do today to get me closer to achieving my next Plan A is:

Start Time: _____ End Time: _____

► The **second** thing I will do today to get me closer to achieving my next Plan A is:

Start Time: ............. End Time: _____

► Today, I will talk with/communicate with Mr./Ms./Dr. _____ about:

## EVENING REFLECTION

► I made ME a priority today by:

► The single most important thing I did today to get me closer to my goals was:

► The one thing that hurt my progress the most today was:

► I will overcome this obstacle tomorrow by:

**199**

## DAY 37, Date:

*If you really want to do something, you will find a way. If you do not, you'll find an excuse.*

**—JIM ROHN,**
*American Entrepreneur*

## MORNING PLANNING

► I choose to have joy today because:

► I am working towards my goal because:

## My Plan A. is:

► The **first** thing I will do today to get me closer to achieving my Plan A. is:

Start Time: _____   End Time: _____

► The **second** thing I will do today to get me closer to achieving my Plan A. is:

Start Time: _____   End Time: _____

## My next plan A is:

_____

_____

► The **first** thing I will do today to get me closer to achieving my next Plan A is:

Start Time: _____ End Time: _____

► The **second** thing I will do today to get me closer to achieving my next Plan A is:

Start Time: _____ End Time: _____

► Today, I will talk with/communicate with Mr./Ms./Dr. _____ about:

## EVENING REFLECTION

► I made ME a priority today by:

► The single most important thing I did today to get me closer to my goals was:

► The one thing that hurt my progress the most today was:

► I will overcome this obstacle tomorrow by:

*You always pass failure on the way to Success.*

—**Mickey Rooney,**
*American Actor*

## MORNING PLANNING

► I choose to have joy today because:

► I am working towards my goal because:

## My Plan A. is:

► The **first** thing I will do today to get me closer to achieving my Plan A. is:

Start Time: _____    End Time: _____

► The **second** thing I will do today to get me closer to achieving my Plan A. is:

Start Time: _____    End Time: _____

## My next plan A is:

_____

_____

► The **first** thing I will do today to get me closer to achieving my next Plan A is:

Start Time: _____ End Time: _____

► The **second** thing I will do today to get me closer to achieving my next Plan A is:

Start Time: _____ End Time: _____

► Today, I will talk with/communicate with Mr./Ms./Dr. _____ about:

## EVENING REFLECTION

► I made ME a priority today by:

► The single most important thing I did today to get me closer to my goals was:

► The one thing that hurt my progress the most today was:

► I will overcome this obstacle tomorrow by:

## DAY 39, Date:

*When I dare to be powerful, to use my strength in the service of my vision, then it becomes less and less important whether I am afraid.*

**— AUDRE LORD,**
*American Writer, Feminist, Womanist, Librarian & Civil Rights Activist*

## MORNING PLANNING

▶ I choose to have joy today because:

▶ I am working towards my goal because:

## My Plan A. is:

► The **first** thing I will do today to get me closer to achieving my Plan A. is:

Start Time: _____     End Time: _____

► The **second** thing I will do today to get me closer to achieving my Plan A. is:

Start Time: _____     End Time: _____

## My next plan A is:

_____

_____

► The **first** thing I will do today to get me closer to achieving my next Plan A is:

Start Time: _____ End Time: _____

► The **second** thing I will do today to get me closer to achieving my next Plan A is:

Start Time: _____ End Time: _____

► Today, I will talk with/communicate with Mr./ Ms./Dr. _____ about:

## EVENING REFLECTION

► I made ME a priority today by:

► The single most important thing I did today to get me closer to my goals was:

► The one thing that hurt my progress the most today was:

► I will overcome this obstacle tomorrow by:

## DAY 40, Date:

*Like art, revolutions come from combining what exists into what has never existed before.*

**—GLORIA STEINEM,**
*American Feminist Journalist & Social Political Activist*

## MORNING PLANNING

► I choose to have joy today because:

► I am working towards my goal because:

## My Plan A. is:

► The **first** thing I will do today to get me closer to achieving my Plan A. is:

Start Time: _____     End Time: _____

► The **second** thing I will do today to get me closer to achieving my Plan A. is:

Start Time: _____     End Time: _____

## My next plan A is:

_____

_____

► The **first** thing I will do today to get me closer to achieving my next Plan A is:

Start Time: _____  End Time: _____

► The **second** thing I will do today to get me closer to achieving my next Plan A is:

Start Time: _____  End Time: _____

► Today, I will talk with/communicate with Mr./Ms./Dr. _____ about:

## EVENING REFLECTION

► I made ME a priority today by:

► The single most important thing I did today to get me closer to my goals was:

► The one thing that hurt my progress the most today was:

► I will overcome this obstacle tomorrow by:

## 5-DAY ACCOUNTABILITY CHECK

*During the past 5 days...*

▶ I made time for my success by:

▶ I increased my knowledge about:

▶ I asked for advice/guidance from:

_____

_____

_____

▶ Over the next 5 days I will talk with/communicate with Mr./Ms./Dr. _____ about:

*The most courageous act is still to think for yourself. Aloud.*

— COCO CHANEL,
*French Fashion Designer & Businesswoman*

## MORNING PLANNING

► I choose to have joy today because:

► I am working towards my goal because:

**My Plan A. is:**

► The **first** thing I will do today to get me closer to achieving my Plan A. is:

Start Time: _____ End Time: _____

► The **second** thing I will do today to get me closer to achieving my Plan A. is:

Start Time: _____ End Time: _____

## My next plan A is:

_____

_____

► The **first** thing I will do today to get me closer to achieving my next Plan A is:

Start Time: _____ End Time: _____

► The **second** thing I will do today to get me closer to achieving my next Plan A is:

Start Time: _____ End Time: _____

► Today, I will talk with/communicate with Mr./Ms./Dr. _____ about:

## EVENING REFLECTION

► I made ME a priority today by:

► The single most important thing I did today to get me closer to my goals was:

► The one thing that hurt my progress the most today was:

► I will overcome this obstacle tomorrow by:

**DAY 42, Date:**

*Strong women aren't simply born. They are made by the storms they walk through.*

—**ANONYMOUS**

## MORNING PLANNING

► I choose to have joy today because:

► I am working towards my goal because:

**My Plan A. is:**

► The **first** thing I will do today to get me closer to achieving my Plan A. is:

Start Time: _____ End Time: _____

► The **second** thing I will do today to get me closer to achieving my Plan A. is:

Start Time: _____ End Time: _____

## My next plan A is:

_____

_____

► The **first** thing I will do today to get me closer to achieving my next Plan A is:

Start Time: _____ End Time: _____

► The **second** thing I will do today to get me closer to achieving my next Plan A is:

Start Time: _____ End Time: _____

► Today, I will talk with/communicate with Mr./ Ms./Dr. _____ about:

## EVENING REFLECTION

► I made ME a priority today by:

► The single most important thing I did today to get me closer to my goals was:

► The one thing that hurt my progress the most today was:

► I will overcome this obstacle tomorrow by:

*I always did something I was a little not ready to do. I think that's how you grow. When there's that moment of 'Wow, I'm not really sure I can do this,' and your push through those moments, that's when you have a breakthrough.*

**—MARISSA MAYER,**
*American Businesswoman & Investor*

## MORNING PLANNING

▶ I choose to have joy today because:

▶ I am working towards my goal because:

**My Plan A. is:**

▶ The **first** thing I will do today to get me closer to achieving my Plan A. is:

Start Time: _____ End Time: _____

▶ The **second** thing I will do today to get me closer to achieving my Plan A. is:

Start Time: _____ End Time: _____

## My next plan A is:

_____

_____

► The **first** thing I will do today to get me closer to achieving my next Plan A is:

Start Time: _____ End Time: _____

► The **second** thing I will do today to get me closer to achieving my next Plan A is:

Start Time: _____ End Time: _____

► Today, I will talk with/communicate with Mr./Ms./Dr. _____ about:

## EVENING REFLECTION

► I made ME a priority today by:

► The single most important thing I did today to get me closer to my goals was:

► The one thing that hurt my progress the most today was:

► I will overcome this obstacle tomorrow by:

## DAY 44, Date:

*The thing women have yet to learn is nobody gives you power. You just take it.*

— ROSEANNE BARR,
*American Actress, Comedian & Producer*

## MORNING PLANNING

► I choose to have joy today because:

► I am working towards my goal because:

## My Plan A. is:

► The **first** thing I will do today to get me closer to achieving my Plan A. is:

Start Time: _____     End Time: _____

► The **second** thing I will do today to get me closer to achieving my Plan A. is:

Start Time: _____     End Time: _____

## My next plan A is:

► The **first** thing I will do today to get me closer to achieving my next Plan A is:

Start Time: _____ End Time: _____

► The **second** thing I will do today to get me closer to achieving my next Plan A is:

Start Time: _____ End Time: _____

► Today, I will talk with/communicate with Mr./Ms./Dr. _____ about:

## EVENING REFLECTION

► I made ME a priority today by:

► The single most important thing I did today to get me closer to my goals was:

► The one thing that hurt my progress the most today was:

► I will overcome this obstacle tomorrow by:

**DAY 45, Date:**

*Beginnings are usually scary, endings are usually sad, but it's what's in the middle that counts.*

—**Steven Rogers,**
*American Screenwriter*

## MORNING PLANNING

► I choose to have joy today because:

► I am working towards my goal because:

**My Plan A. is:**

► The **first** thing I will do today to get me closer to achieving my Plan A. is:

Start Time: _____    End Time: _____

► The **second** thing I will do today to get me closer to achieving my Plan A. is:

Start Time: _____    End Time: _____

## My next plan A is:

_____

_____

► The **first** thing I will do today to get me closer to achieving my next Plan A is:

Start Time: _____ End Time: _____

► The **second** thing I will do today to get me closer to achieving my next Plan A is:

Start Time: _____ End Time: _____

► Today, I will talk with/communicate with Mr./ Ms./Dr. _____ about:

## EVENING REFLECTION

► I made ME a priority today by:

► The single most important thing I did today to get me closer to my goals was:

► The one thing that hurt my progress the most today was:

► I will overcome this obstacle tomorrow by:

## 5-DAY ACCOUNTABILITY CHECK

*During the past 5 days...*

▶ I made time for my success by:

▶ I increased my knowledge about:

▶ I asked for advice/guidance from:

_____

_____

_____

▶ Over the next 5 days I will talk with/communicate
with Mr./Ms./Dr. _____ about:

## 3 BOOKS TO EMPOWER YOU

► *Year of Yes: How to Dance It Out, Stand in the Sun and Be Your Own Person* by Shonda Rhimes

► *Raving Fans* by Kenneth H. Blanchard & Sheldon Bowles

► *Atomic Habits: An Easy & Proven Way to Build Good Habits & Break Bad Ones* by James Clear

*Never be ashamed of what you feel. You have the right to feel any emotion that you want, and to do what makes you happy. That's my life motto.*

—DEMI LOVATO,
*American Singer, Songwriter & Actress*

## MORNING PLANNING

► I choose to have joy today because:

► I am working towards my goal because:

**My Plan A. is:**

► The **first** thing I will do today to get me closer to achieving my Plan A. is:

Start Time: _____     End Time: _____

► The **second** thing I will do today to get me closer to achieving my Plan A. is:

Start Time: _____     End Time: _____

## My next plan A is:

_____

_____

► The **first** thing I will do today to get me closer to achieving my next Plan A is:

Start Time: _____ End Time: _____

► The **second** thing I will do today to get me closer to achieving my next Plan A is:

Start Time: _____ End Time: _____

► Today, I will talk with/communicate with Mr./Ms./Dr. _____ about:

## EVENING REFLECTION

► I made ME a priority today by:

► The single most important thing I did today to get me closer to my goals was:

► The one thing that hurt my progress the most today was:

► I will overcome this obstacle tomorrow by:

*It's not what happens to you, but how you react to it that matters.*

—**EPICTETUS,**
*Greek Philosopher*

## MORNING PLANNING

▶  I choose to have joy today because:

▶  I am working towards my goal because:

**My Plan A. is:**

► The **first** thing I will do today to get me closer to achieving my Plan A. is:

Start Time: _____ End Time: _____

► The **second** thing I will do today to get me closer to achieving my Plan A. is:

Start Time: _____ End Time: _____

## My next plan A is:

_____

_____

► The **first** thing I will do today to get me closer to achieving my next Plan A is:

Start Time: _____ End Time: _____

► The **second** thing I will do today to get me closer to achieving my next Plan A is:

Start Time: _____ End Time: _____

► Today, I will talk with/communicate with Mr./Ms./Dr. _____ about:

## EVENING REFLECTION

▶ I made ME a priority today by:

▶ The single most important thing I did today to get me closer to my goals was:

▶ The one thing that hurt my progress the most today was:

▶ I will overcome this obstacle tomorrow by:

*Only surround yourself with people who will lift you higher.*

**—OPRAH WINFREY,**
*Television Producer, Actress, Author, Philanthropist, Host*

## MORNING PLANNING

► I choose to have joy today because:

► I am working towards my goal because:

**My Plan A. is:**

► The **first** thing I will do today to get me closer to achieving my Plan A. is:

Start Time: _____     End Time: _____

► The **second** thing I will do today to get me closer to achieving my Plan A. is:

Start Time: _____     End Time: _____

## My next plan A is:

_____

_____

► The **first** thing I will do today to get me closer to achieving my next Plan A is:

Start Time: _____ End Time: _____

► The **second** thing I will do today to get me closer to achieving my next Plan A is:

Start Time: _____ End Time: _____

► Today, I will talk with/communicate with Mr./Ms./Dr. _____ about:

## EVENING REFLECTION

► I made ME a priority today by:

► The single most important thing I did today to get me closer to my goals was:

► The one thing that hurt my progress the most today was:

► I will overcome this obstacle tomorrow by:

**DAY 49, Date:**

*Women have to harness their power—it's absolutely true. It's just learning not to take the first no. And if you can't go straight, you go around the corner.*

— **CHER,**
*American Singer & Actress*

## MORNING PLANNING

► I choose to have joy today because:

► I am working towards my goal because:

**My Plan A. is:**

► The **first** thing I will do today to get me closer to achieving my Plan A. is:

Start Time: _____    End Time: _____

► The **second** thing I will do today to get me closer to achieving my Plan A. is:

Start Time: _____    End Time: _____

## My next plan A is:

_____

_____

► The **first** thing I will do today to get me closer to achieving my next Plan A is:

Start Time: _____ End Time: _____

► The **second** thing I will do today to get me closer to achieving my next Plan A is:

Start Time: _____ End Time: _____

► Today, I will talk with/communicate with Mr./Ms./Dr. _____ about:

## EVENING REFLECTION

► I made ME a priority today by:

► The single most important thing I did today to get me closer to my goals was:

► The one thing that hurt my progress the most today was:

► I will overcome this obstacle tomorrow by:

*I'm learning how to drown out the constant noise that is such an inseparable part of my life. I don't have to prove anything to anyone. I only have to follow my heart and concentrate on what I want to say to the world. I run my world.*

—BEYONCÉ,
*American Singer, Actress & Businesswoman*

## MORNING PLANNING

▶ I choose to have joy today because:

▶ I am working towards my goal because:

## My Plan A. is:

► The **first** thing I will do today to get me closer to achieving my Plan A. is:

Start Time: _____ End Time: _____

► The **second** thing I will do today to get me closer to achieving my Plan A. is:

Start Time: _____ End Time: _____

## My next plan A is:

_____

_____

► The **first** thing I will do today to get me closer to achieving my next Plan A is:

Start Time: _____     End Time: _____

► The **second** thing I will do today to get me closer to achieving my next Plan A is:

Start Time: _____     End Time: _____

► Today, I will talk with/communicate with Mr./ Ms./Dr. _____ about:

## EVENING REFLECTION

► I made ME a priority today by:

► The single most important thing I did today to get me closer to my goals was:

► The one thing that hurt my progress the most today was:

► I will overcome this obstacle tomorrow by:

## 5-DAY ACCOUNTABILITY CHECK

*During the past 5 days...*

► I made time for my success by:

► I increased my knowledge about:

► I asked for advice/guidance from:

_____

_____

_____

► Over the next 5 days I will talk with/communicate with Mr./Ms./Dr. _____ about:

**260**

*There's something so special about a woman who dominates in a man's world. It takes a certain grace, strength intelligence, fearlessness, and the nerve to never take no for an answer.*

—**RIHANNA,**
*Barbadian Singer, Actress, Fashion Designer & Businesswoman*

## MORNING PLANNING

▶ I choose to have joy today because:

▶ I am working towards my goal because:

**My Plan A. is:**

► The **first** thing I will do today to get me closer to achieving my Plan A. is:

Start Time: _____     End Time: _____

► The **second** thing I will do today to get me closer to achieving my Plan A. is:

Start Time: _____     End Time: _____

## My next plan A is:

_____

_____

► The **first** thing I will do today to get me closer to achieving my next Plan A is:

Start Time: _____     End Time: _____

► The **second** thing I will do today to get me closer to achieving my next Plan A is:

Start Time: _____     End Time: _____

► Today, I will talk with/communicate with Mr./Ms./Dr. _____ about:

## EVENING REFLECTION

► I made ME a priority today by:

► The single most important thing I did today to get me closer to my goals was:

► The one thing that hurt my progress the most today was:

► I will overcome this obstacle tomorrow by:

## DAY 52, Date:

*As women, we have to start appreciating our own worth and each other's worth. Seek out strong women to befriend, to align yourself with, to learn from, to collaborate with, to be inspired by, to support, and be enlightened by.*

—MADONNA,
*American Signer, Songwriter & Actress*

## MORNING PLANNING

► I choose to have joy today because:

► I am working towards my goal because:

## My Plan A. is:

▶ The **first** thing I will do today to get me closer to achieving my Plan A. is:

Start Time: _____        End Time: _____

▶ The **second** thing I will do today to get me closer to achieving my Plan A. is:

Start Time: _____        End Time: _____

## My next plan A is:

► The **first** thing I will do today to get me closer to achieving my next Plan A is:

Start Time: _____     End Time: _____

► The **second** thing I will do today to get me closer to achieving my next Plan A is:

Start Time: _____     End Time: _____

► Today, I will talk with/communicate with Mr./Ms./Dr. _____ about:

## EVENING REFLECTION

▶ I made ME a priority today by:

▶ The single most important thing I did today to get me closer to my goals was:

▶ The one thing that hurt my progress the most today was:

▶ I will overcome this obstacle tomorrow by:

*No one can make you feel inferior without your consent.*

—**ELEANOR ROOSEVELT,**
*Former First Lady of the United States*

## MORNING PLANNING

▶ I choose to have joy today because:

▶ I am working towards my goal because:

**My Plan A. is:**

► The **first** thing I will do today to get me closer to achieving my Plan A. is:

Start Time: _____    End Time: _____

► The **second** thing I will do today to get me closer to achieving my Plan A. is:

Start Time: _____    End Time: _____

## My next plan A is:

_____

_____

► The **first** thing I will do today to get me closer to achieving my next Plan A is:

Start Time: _____ End Time: _____

► The **second** thing I will do today to get me closer to achieving my next Plan A is:

Start Time: _____ End Time: _____

► Today, I will talk with/communicate with Mr./Ms./Dr. _____ about:

## EVENING REFLECTION

► I made ME a priority today by:

► The single most important thing I did today to get me closer to my goals was:

► The one thing that hurt my progress the most today was:

► I will overcome this obstacle tomorrow by:

*I have learned that as long as I hold fast to my beliefs and values—and follow my own moral compass—then the only expectations I need to live up to are my own.*

— MICHELLE OBAMA,
*Former First Lady of the United States of America*

## MORNING PLANNING

► I choose to have joy today because:

► I am working towards my goal because:

**My Plan A. is:**

► The **first** thing I will do today to get me closer to achieving my Plan A. is:

Start Time: _____     End Time: _____

► The **second** thing I will do today to get me closer to achieving my Plan A. is:

Start Time: _____     End Time: _____

## My next plan A is:

_____

_____

► The **first** thing I will do today to get me closer to achieving my next Plan A is:

Start Time: _____ End Time: _____

► The **second** thing I will do today to get me closer to achieving my next Plan A is:

Start Time: _____ End Time: _____

► Today, I will talk with/communicate with Mr./ Ms./Dr. _____ about:

## EVENING REFLECTION

► I made ME a priority today by:

► The single most important thing I did today to get me closer to my goals was:

► The one thing that hurt my progress the most today was:

► I will overcome this obstacle tomorrow by:

*We do not need magic to transform our world. We carry all of the power we need inside ourselves already.*

**—J.K. ROWLING,**
*British Author, Philanthropist,
Film Producer & Screenwriter*

## MORNING PLANNING

► I choose to have joy today because:

► I am working towards my goal because:

**My Plan A. is:**

► The **first** thing I will do today to get me closer to achieving my Plan A. is:

Start Time: _____    End Time: _____

► The **second** thing I will do today to get me closer to achieving my Plan A. is:

Start Time: _____    End Time: _____

## My next plan A is:

_____

_____

► The **first** thing I will do today to get me closer to achieving my next Plan A is:

Start Time: _____    End Time: _____

► The **second** thing I will do today to get me closer to achieving my next Plan A is:

Start Time: _____    End Time: _____

► Today, I will talk with/communicate with Mr./Ms./Dr. _____ about:

## EVENING REFLECTION

▶ I made ME a priority today by:

▶ The single most important thing I did today to get me closer to my goals was:

▶ The one thing that hurt my progress the most today was:

▶ I will overcome this obstacle tomorrow by:

## 5-DAY ACCOUNTABILITY CHECK

*During the past 5 days...*

▶  I made time for my success by:

▶  I increased my knowledge about:

▶  I asked for advice/guidance from:

_____

_____

_____

▶  Over the next 5 days I will talk with/communicate
   with Mr./Ms./Dr. _____ about:

*The moment you let your yesterdays control your tomorrows is the moment your soul dies, because it cannot move forward living in the past.*

—**POETIC EVOLUTION,**
*Author*

## MORNING PLANNING

► I choose to have joy today because:

► I am working towards my goal because:

**My Plan A. is:**

► The **first** thing I will do today to get me closer to achieving my Plan A. is:

Start Time: _____     End Time: _____

► The **second** thing I will do today to get me closer to achieving my Plan A. is:

Start Time: _____     End Time: _____

## My next plan A is:

_____

_____

► The **first** thing I will do today to get me closer to achieving my next Plan A is:

Start Time: _____     End Time: _____

► The **second** thing I will do today to get me closer to achieving my next Plan A is:

Start Time: _____     End Time: _____

► Today, I will talk with/communicate with Mr./Ms./Dr. _____ about:

## EVENING REFLECTION

► I made ME a priority today by:

► The single most important thing I did today to get me closer to my goals was:

► The one thing that hurt my progress the most today was:

► I will overcome this obstacle tomorrow by:

*No one ever became a success without taking chances...one must be able to recognize the moment and seize it without delay.*

**—ESTÉE LAUDER,**
*American Businesswoman*

## MORNING PLANNING

► I choose to have joy today because:

► I am working towards my goal because:

**My Plan A. is:**

► The **first** thing I will do today to get me closer to achieving my Plan A. is:

Start Time: _____ End Time: _____

► The **second** thing I will do today to get me closer to achieving my Plan A. is:

Start Time: _____ End Time: _____

## My next plan A is:

_____

_____

► The **first** thing I will do today to get me closer to achieving my next Plan A is:

Start Time: _____ End Time: _____

► The **second** thing I will do today to get me closer to achieving my next Plan A is:

Start Time: _____ End Time: _____

► Today, I will talk with/communicate with Mr./ Ms./Dr. _____ about:

## EVENING REFLECTION

► I made ME a priority today by:

► The single most important thing I did today to get me closer to my goals was:

► The one thing that hurt my progress the most today was:

► I will overcome this obstacle tomorrow by:

*Find something you're passionate about and keep tremendously interested in it.*

**—JULIA CHILD,**
*American Cooking Teacher,*
*Author & Television Personality*

## MORNING PLANNING

▶ I choose to have joy today because:

▶ I am working towards my goal because:

**My Plan A. is:**

► The **first** thing I will do today to get me closer to achieving my Plan A. is:

Start Time: _____    End Time: _____

► The **second** thing I will do today to get me closer to achieving my Plan A. is:

Start Time: _____    End Time: _____

## My next plan A is:

_____

_____

► The **first** thing I will do today to get me closer to achieving my next Plan A is:

Start Time: _____   End Time: _____

► The **second** thing I will do today to get me closer to achieving my next Plan A is:

Start Time: _____   End Time: _____

► Today, I will talk with/communicate with Mr./Ms./Dr. _____ about:

## EVENING REFLECTION

► I made ME a priority today by:

► The single most important thing I did today to get me closer to my goals was:

► The one thing that hurt my progress the most today was:

► I will overcome this obstacle tomorrow by:

*There's no elevator to Success. You have to take the stairs.*

— UNKNOWN

## MORNING PLANNING

► I choose to have joy today because:

► I am working towards my goal because:

**My Plan A. is:**

► The **first** thing I will do today to get me closer to achieving my Plan A. is:

Start Time: _____     End Time: _____

► The **second** thing I will do today to get me closer to achieving my Plan A. is:

Start Time: _____     End Time: _____

## My next plan A is:

_____

_____

► The **first** thing I will do today to get me closer to achieving my next Plan A is:

Start Time: _____  End Time: _____

► The **second** thing I will do today to get me closer to achieving my next Plan A is:

Start Time: _____  End Time: _____

► Today, I will talk with/communicate with Mr./ Ms./Dr. _____ about:

## EVENING REFLECTION

► I made ME a priority today by:

► The single most important thing I did today to get me closer to my goals was:

► The one thing that hurt my progress the most today was:

► I will overcome this obstacle tomorrow by:

*Think like a queen. A queen is not afraid to fail. Failure is another stepping-stone to greatness.*

—**OPRAH WINFREY,**
*Television Producer, Actress, Author, Philanthropist, Host*

## MORNING PLANNING

▶ I choose to have joy today because:

▶ I am working towards my goal because:

**My Plan A. is:**

► The **first** thing I will do today to get me closer to achieving my Plan A. is:

Start Time: _____    End Time: _____

► The **second** thing I will do today to get me closer to achieving my Plan A. is:

Start Time: _____    End Time: _____

## My next plan A is:

► The **first** thing I will do today to get me closer to achieving my next Plan A is:

Start Time: _____ End Time: _____

► The **second** thing I will do today to get me closer to achieving my next Plan A is:

Start Time: _____ End Time: _____

► Today, I will talk with/communicate with Mr./ Ms./Dr. _____ about:

## EVENING REFLECTION

▶ I made ME a priority today by:

▶ The single most important thing I did today to get me closer to my goals was:

▶ The one thing that hurt my progress the most today was:

▶ I will overcome this obstacle tomorrow by:

## 5-DAY ACCOUNTABILITY CHECK

*During the past 5 days...*

▶ I made time for my success by:

▶ I increased my knowledge about:

▶ I asked for advice/guidance from:

_____

_____

_____

▶ Over the next 5 days I will talk with/communicate
with Mr./Ms./Dr. _____ about:

*"If they obey and serve Him, they shall spend their days in prosperity, and their years in pleasures."*

—JOB 36:11

## MORNING PLANNING

▶ I choose to have joy today because:

▶ I am working towards my goal because:

**My Plan A. is:**

► The **first** thing I will do today to get me closer to achieving my Plan A. is:

Start Time: _____ End Time: _____

► The **second** thing I will do today to get me closer to achieving my Plan A. is:

Start Time: _____ End Time: _____

## My next plan A is:

_____

_____

▶ The **first** thing I will do today to get me closer to achieving my next Plan A is:

Start Time: _____    End Time: _____

▶ The **second** thing I will do today to get me closer to achieving my next Plan A is:

Start Time: _____    End Time: _____

▶ Today, I will talk with/communicate with Mr./Ms./Dr. _____ about:

## EVENING REFLECTION

▶ I made ME a priority today by:

▶ The single most important thing I did today to get me closer to my goals was:

▶ The one thing that hurt my progress the most today was:

▶ I will overcome this obstacle tomorrow by:

*If you're one of those people who has that little voice in the back of her mind saying, 'Maybe I could do [fill in the blank]', don't tell it to be quiet. Give it a little room to grow and try to find an environment it can grow in.*

—**REESE WITHERSPOON,**
*American Actress, Producer & Entrepreneur*

## MORNING PLANNING

► I choose to have joy today because:

► I am working towards my goal because:

**My Plan A. is:**

► The **first** thing I will do today to get me closer to achieving my Plan A. is:

Start Time: _____     End Time: _____

► The **second** thing I will do today to get me closer to achieving my Plan A. is:

Start Time: _____     End Time: _____

## My next plan A is:

_____

_____

► The **first** thing I will do today to get me closer to achieving my next Plan A is:

Start Time: _____ End Time: _____

► The **second** thing I will do today to get me closer to achieving my next Plan A is:

Start Time: _____ End Time: _____

► Today, I will talk with/communicate with Mr./ Ms./Dr. _____ about:

## EVENING REFLECTION

► I made ME a priority today by:

► The single most important thing I did today to get me closer to my goals was:

► The one thing that hurt my progress the most today was:

► I will overcome this obstacle tomorrow by:

*If you want to run for Prime Minister, you can. If you don't, that's wonderful, too. Shave your armpits, don't shave them, wear flats one day, heels the next. These things are so irrelevant and surface to what it is all really about, and I wish people wouldn't get caught up in that. We want to empower women to do exactly what they want, to be true to themselves, to have the opportunities to develop. Women should feel free.*

—EMMA WATSON,
*English Actress & Activist*

## MORNING PLANNING

► I choose to have joy today because:

► I am working towards my goal because:

## My Plan A. is:

_____

_____

► The **first** thing I will do today to get me closer to achieving my Plan A. is:

Start Time: _____     End Time: _____

► The **second** thing I will do today to get me closer to achieving my Plan A. is:

Start Time: _____     End Time: _____

## My next plan A is:

_____

_____

▶ The **first** thing I will do today to get me closer to achieving my next Plan A is:

Start Time: _____     End Time: _____

▶ The **second** thing I will do today to get me closer to achieving my next Plan A is:

Start Time: _____     End Time: _____

▶ Today, I will talk with/communicate with Mr./Ms./Dr. _____ about:

## EVENING REFLECTION

► I made ME a priority today by:

► The single most important thing I did today to get me closer to my goals was:

► The one thing that hurt my progress the most today was:

► I will overcome this obstacle tomorrow by:

## DAY 64, Date:

*You could certainly say that I've never underestimated myself. There's nothing wrong with being ambitious.*

— **ANGELA MERKEL**,
*German Politician*

## MORNING PLANNING

▶ I choose to have joy today because:

▶ I am working towards my goal because:

## My Plan A. is:

► The **first** thing I will do today to get me closer to achieving my Plan A. is:

Start Time: _____     End Time: _____

► The **second** thing I will do today to get me closer to achieving my Plan A. is:

Start Time: _____     End Time: _____

## My next plan A is:

_____

_____

► The **first** thing I will do today to get me closer to achieving my next Plan A is:

Start Time: _____  End Time: _____

► The **second** thing I will do today to get me closer to achieving my next Plan A is:

Start Time: _____  End Time: _____

► Today, I will talk with/communicate with Mr./Ms./Dr. _____ about:

## EVENING REFLECTION

► I made ME a priority today by:

► The single most important thing I did today to get me closer to my goals was:

► The one thing that hurt my progress the most today was:

► I will overcome this obstacle tomorrow by:

*There is a stubbornness about me that can never bear to be frightened at the will of others. My courage always rises at every attempt to intimidate me.*

—**JANE AUSTEN,** *English Novelist*

## MORNING PLANNING

► I choose to have joy today because:

► I am working towards my goal because:

## My Plan A. is:

► The **first** thing I will do today to get me closer to achieving my Plan A. is:

Start Time: _____    End Time: _____

► The **second** thing I will do today to get me closer to achieving my Plan A. is:

Start Time: _____    End Time: _____

## My next plan A is:

_____

_____

► The **first** thing I will do today to get me closer to achieving my next Plan A is:

Start Time: _____     End Time: _____

► The **second** thing I will do today to get me closer to achieving my next Plan A is:

Start Time: _____     End Time: _____

► Today, I will talk with/communicate with Mr./Ms./Dr. _____ about:

## EVENING REFLECTION

► I made ME a priority today by:

► The single most important thing I did today to get me closer to my goals was:

► The one thing that hurt my progress the most today was:

► I will overcome this obstacle tomorrow by:

## 5-DAY ACCOUNTABILITY CHECK

*During the past 5 days...*

► I made time for my success by:

► I increased my knowledge about:

► I asked for advice/guidance from:

_____

_____

_____

► Over the next 5 days I will talk with/communicate
with Mr./Ms./Dr. _____ about:

*Happiness, good health, success… this is the return on investing in yourself first.*

—DR. J.K. ELLIS,
*Businesswoman & Investor*

## MORNING PLANNING

► I choose to have joy today because:

► I am working towards my goal because:

**My Plan A. is:**

► The **first** thing I will do today to get me closer to achieving my Plan A. is:

Start Time: _____ End Time: _____

► The **second** thing I will do today to get me closer to achieving my Plan A. is:

Start Time: _____ End Time: _____

## My next plan A is:

_____

_____

► The **first** thing I will do today to get me closer to achieving my next Plan A is:

Start Time: _____ End Time: _____

► The **second** thing I will do today to get me closer to achieving my next Plan A is:

Start Time: _____ End Time: _____

► Today, I will talk with/communicate with Mr./Ms./Dr. _____ about:

## EVENING REFLECTION

► I made ME a priority today by:

► The single most important thing I did today to get me closer to my goals was:

► The one thing that hurt my progress the most today was:

► I will overcome this obstacle tomorrow by:

# CONGRATULATIONS!

**Y**ou have Successfully stuck to writing down and executing your goals for 66 days. Whatever your Plan A's are, you should have achieved them by now. If you haven't, that is okay too because you have made great progress towards reaching your Success. This journey was more about you developing the good habits of writing down your goals and working to achieve them daily. It was less about you actually reaching them. If you have learned how to write your plan down daily and work each day towards the Success you want and deserve, you have already been Successful. Continuing to do this will ensure that you reach any goal you set for yourself. You have developed Success as a habit.

*Always remember that it is your job to <u>Motivate</u>, Inspire, and <u>EMPOWER</u> yourself to the Success you want and deserve.*

# Focused Thoughts & Notes

## Focused Thoughts & Notes

## Focused Thoughts & Notes

# Focused Thoughts & Notes

# Focused Thoughts & Notes

www.ingramcontent.com/pod-product-compliance
Lightning Source LLC
Chambersburg PA
CBHW060858120626
46553CB00001B/127